THE TRIPLE HAPPINESS

Brooke Berman

BROADWAY PLAY PUBLISHING INC
224 E 62nd St, NY NY 10065-8201
212 772-8334 fax: 212 772-8358
BroadwayPlayPubl.com

THE TRIPLE HAPPINESS
© Copyright 2010 by Brooke Berman

First printing: October 2010
I S B N: 978-0-88145-446-X

Book design: Marie Donovan
Typographic controls: Adobe InDesign
Typeface: Palatino
Printed and bound in the U S A

ABOUT THE AUTHOR

Brooke Berman's plays have been produced and developed across the U S at theaters including: Primary Stages, The Second Stage, Steppenwolf, The Play Company, Soho Rep, Williamstown Theater Festival, Naked Angels, M C C, WET, S P F, New Dramatists, New Georges, The Hourglass Group and the Eugene O'Neill Theater Center. In the U K, her work has been developed at The Royal Court Theatre, The National Theatre Studio and Pentabus. Plays include: HUNTING AND GATHERING (Primary Stages, named one of the 10 Best Plays of 2008 by *New York Magazine*); SMASHING (The Play Company, The O'Neill); UNTIL WE FIND EACH OTHER (Steppenwolf, The O'Neill); THE TRIPLE HAPPINESS (Second Stage, The Playwrights Center, The Hourglass Group), SAM AND LUCY (S P F, Cleveland Playhouse), A PERFECT COUPLE (WET), OUT OF THE WATER (Cape Cod Theater Project, ARS Nova), THE JESUS YEAR (New Dramatists Creativity Fund), THE LIDDY PLAYS (Rising Phoenix Rep, The Hangar Theater Lab, Williamstown Theater Company), and others.

Brooke is the recipient of a Berilla Kerr Award, a Helen Merrill Award, two Francesca Primus Awards, two LeCompte du Nuoy awards and a commissioning grant from the National Foundation for Jewish Culture. She is an alumna of New Dramatists, where she served on the Board of Directors and developed countless plays. She has received support for her work from the MacDowell Colony and the Corporation of Yaddo and commissions from Arielle Tepper Productions and C T C in Minneapolis.

Her short play DANCING WITH A DEVIL was a co-winner of The Heideman Award at Actors Theater of Louisville in 1999, presented in *Life Under 30* at the Humana Festival, and nominated for an American Theater Critics Best New Play award. It has been published in numerous anthologies. Her short play DEFUSION has been produced in a number of festivals and as part of Christine Jones's Theater for One project at New York Theatre Workshop. (www.theatreforone. com/gallery/img_0470.htm)

Brooke attended Barnard College and is a graduate of The Juilliard School. She is a member of the Dramatists Guild, PEN and the M C C Playwrights Coalition.

Her memoir, *No Place Like Home*, is published by Random House and available in bookstores. More information: www.brookeberman.net.

THE TRIPLE HAPPINESS was originally developed through Soho Rep Writer/Director Lab and received additional development and support through ASK Theater Projects, The Royal Court Theatre in London, and the Playwrights Center in Minneapolis.

THE TRIPLE HAPPINESS had additional development by The Hourglass Group (Elyse Singer, Artistic Director) as part of a reading series at the Gershwin and on a Summer Development Retreat at Choate Rosemary Hall. The Hourglass Group then did a workshop production opening on 31 March 2001. The cast and creative contributors were:

MIKE .... Bryant Richards
JAMIE... Richard Barboza
HOPE... Nina Hellman
LIZ..Susan Knight
STAN ....Tibor Feldman
TESSA ....Jan Leslie Harding

Director...Elyse Singer
Set/lighting ....Kip Marsh
Costumes... Angela Kahler
Stage manager..Terry Dale

THE TRIPLE HAPPINESS was subsequently produced
by Second Stage. The cast and creative contributors
were:

MIKE .... Keith Nobbs
JAMIE..Jesse J Perez
HOPE.. Marin Ireland
LIZ...Betsy Aidem
STAN ....Mark Blum
TESSA .... Ally Sheedy

Director.. Michael John Garces
Costumes.. Miranda Hoffman
Lighting.. Ben Stanton
Sets.. Andromache Chalfant

AUTHORS NOTE

This is a magical play about a shift in perception. It is not and was never meant to be a naturalistic play about a family in Larchmont, but rather, the choice that each character makes regarding her own precious, creative energy. The play asks, Which world do you want to live in? Are you here to participate in a world full of dead values? Or are you here to create something better?

Although the characters traffic in longing, the play is positive and enthusiastic, urging each to get unstuck. Productions should focus more on this blatant offer ("I'm going to live in the New World. Want to come?") than on the family drama. Don't get mired in the mess.

The play is constructed musically; it should move like music.

Characters say what they mean at all times, devoid of subtext – but also, while they mean what they say entirely at the moment they say it, they might also change their minds later. Complicated thoughts are easily articulated. The language surges forward, infused with the desire to connect. Each of these characters speak with relentless desire to connect.

Regarding the "real" and the "unreal": for the actor, everything is real at all times. There is a real boy named Mike who really sits next to Hope in class and really lives in Larchmont, New York. And also, there is a girl named Hope writing this entire story. The ability to create is what sets her free and separates her from the other characters. Let everything be real, and also, nothing. It is a story. All stories are equally real and unreal.

"...if you go back, you will release energy into what is being decomposed. If you go forward, you will assist in the rebuilding ... The level of consciousness supports your intention in every minute."

—*Sunlight On Water*

ACT ONE

coming home

(MIKE *and* JAMIE, *two young men on a bus.* MIKE *is eighteen.* JAMIE *is in his late twenties.* MIKE *likes to talk to strangers.*)

MIKE: Are you going home?

JAMIE: Hmm?

MIKE: You are, aren't you? I am. I'm going home.

JAMIE: Yeah, sort of. I'm sort of going home.

MIKE: Yeah. I could tell. Me too.

JAMIE: Oh?

MIKE: Sure. To my parents. For the break.

JAMIE: What break?

MIKE: Semester break. The break between semesters. Which happens to correspond with the major holidays of Christmas, sometimes Chanukah and always New Years. But it isn't about the holidays, per se, so much as about the break itself.

JAMIE: I see.

MIKE: And you? Who are you going home to?

JAMIE: Someone special.

MIKE: A girl?

JAMIE: Yeah. A girl.

MIKE: I knew it. You look like you're going home to a girl.

JAMIE: Yeah? What else do I look like?

MIKE: You've been gone a long time.

JAMIE: I've been gone a year.

MIKE: I've just been at school. I've been gone a few months. And I talk to them all the time. All the time. The 'rents. We're really close.

JAMIE: Yeah?

MIKE: Yeah.

JAMIE: That must be nice.

MIKE: It is. Nice. I guess. I mean, I think, yeah I think it's nice. Sure. I mean. We all really like each other and talk and communicate. That's nice. Isn't it?

JAMIE: It's nice.

MIKE: My parents live just outside New York. Is your girlfriend in Manhattan?

JAMIE: Chinatown.

MIKE: Really? I love Chinatown. I used to go a bar there when I was in high school. The Triple Happiness. I liked the name. I do lots of things because of names. I like words. Do you like words?

JAMIE: I've been to that bar.

MIKE: Really? It's a great bar. It's this place that you don't know exists 'til you've been there and then, even after you've been there, you can never find it again.

JAMIE: It's not marked.

MIKE: Exactly. But that's what's so cool about it. I mean, I have no idea how to get there. My friend always led me. He knew where it was. Do you know where it is?

JAMIE: More or less.

MIKE: Yeah, I guess you would. I mean, you're right around there all the time. Of course you know where it is. Oh, hey, my name's Mike. What's yours?

(Lights up on STAN *and* LIZ *in Larchmont, an affluent, "white collar" suburb of New York.)*

LIZ: He said his bus gets in at twelve. He gets a train from the City, and he'll be home in no time. By two, certainly. And that's including if he stops for ice cream or soup or a newspaper or something.

STAN: They have ice cream and soup and newspapers at that college of his. They have those things there. It's not remote or anything.

LIZ: But he's home. Boys like to do things like that when they come home. They need to wander around before showing up. Don't you remember *Catcher in the Rye?*

STAN: That's not what I remember from *Catcher in the Rye.*

LIZ: Holden Caulfield needed to wander around a bit.

STAN: Liz. Our son is not Holden Caulfield. He's just our son.

LIZ: Okay. He's just our son. But I think he's going to wander around a bit. I certainly would.

(And now we watch both scenes as they shift in and out of focus.)

MIKE: I'm going to be a writer. That's why I'm talking to you right now. I am interested in peoples' stories. I have this goal. I'm going to collect stories over the break, as many as I can.

JAMIE: Yeah?

MIKE: Yeah.

JAMIE: Then what? What are you gonna do once they're collected?

MIKE: Oh. (*He hasn't thought of this part yet.*) I don't know. I mean, sure, of course I'll do something with them....

JAMIE: You could write about them.

MIKE: Yeah. I could do that. I mean, of course that's what I'll do. If I'm gonna be a writer, I should do that.

JAMIE: It makes sense.

MIKE: Will you tell me yours?

JAMIE: My what?

MIKE: Your story. What's happened to you. Who you are. What you alone have seen. Come on. You can't say "no."

JAMIE: You want to hear my story?

MIKE: Yes, I do.

JAMIE: No fucking way.

MIKE: Come on...

JAMIE: No way. Too personal. Lots of adult themes. You're not ready for my story, Kid.

MIKE: Please?

LIZ: We need to buy food.

(STAN *ignores her.*)

LIZ: Could you?

STAN: Could I what??

LIZ: Buy food.

STAN: What kind of food?

LIZ: Get what Mike eats. We already have what we eat. Just get what he eats.

STAN: What does he eat?

LIZ: I don't know. He's been at school.

STAN: You go. I don't know what he eats. Could you go?

LIZ: I could go.

(Beat)

STAN: What!?

LIZ: Nothing.

MIKE: So lets start with the basics. What do you do?

JAMIE: What do you mean what do I do?

MIKE: What do you do?

JAMIE: I don't do anything.

MIKE: Sure you do. You've got to do something.

JAMIE: Well. I travel.

MIKE: That's it?

JAMIE: Just about.

MIKE: Oh.

JAMIE: Isn't that enough for you?

MIKE: Sure.

JAMIE: I travel. Think about things. I think about a lot of things. Mull them over. In my mind. I have experiences. I meet people.

MIKE: How do you pay for this? Are you independently wealthy?

JAMIE: Uh, no. I get jobs here and there. But I'm not trying to be anything. Not like you. Not like a writer.

I just want to live. Here and there. I just want to live.
Liquid-like. Keeping things liquid and fluid. Liquid
and fluid. You got that?

MIKE: What does your girlfriend think about that?

JAMIE: She's not my girlfriend.

MIKE: Oh. Is that why?

JAMIE: None of your fucking business.

MIKE: Sorry.

JAMIE: Besides, it doesn't even matter if she's my
girlfriend. We're on a deeper level than that. It doesn't
even matter.

MIKE: That she's not your girlfriend?

JAMIE: She's still my girl.

MIKE: I don't get it. How can she be not your girlfriend
but still Your Girl?

(JAMIE *looks at* MIKE *like he will kill him.*)

MIKE: Is this one of the adult themes?

(JAMIE *looks even more like he will kill* MIKE —)

JAMIE: (*Breaking it down for* MIKE) Okay. Let me try to
explain something. My girl. Candy—

MIKE: Her name is Candy?

JAMIE: Do you want to hear this or not?

(MIKE *nods and obediently shuts up.*)

JAMIE: Okay. Candy—my girl—is the person I love.
There is this thing between us, and it's a kind of love.
The kind that runs so deep you can't do anything
about it, you can't even really live in it, you just have
to stare. It is the love that makes everything else crash.
It freaks me out, makes me sick, I have to run away
from it sometimes. So I travel. And so she is not my

girlfriend. But she is the other piece of me. She is the piece that makes my heart real.

MIKE: Wow. Do you think I'll ever feel anything like that? For anyone?

JAMIE: No. Probably not.

MIKE: Oh.

JAMIE: I don't think it's too common.

MIKE: My parents don't have that kind of love. My friends' parents either. I bet the Fitzgeralds did. I bet that Dostoyevsky did too. I mean, I don't know anything about Dostoyevsky, but I bet that to write like that you either have to have that kind of love you describe, or else, just die lonely. Dying lonely makes good writing too. I don't know many people who have that kind of love, though.

JAMIE: Like I said. It's not common. And it hurts like a motherfucker. Maybe you're better off without it.

LIZ: This will be good.

STAN: (*Not listening*) Sure.

LIZ: We'll get to know each other.

STAN: Of course.

LIZ: Are you listening?

STAN: I hate when you do this.

LIZ: What am I doing?

STAN: We know each other, Liz. We're a fucking family. Families know each other. We have the same genes, Liz. What is there to know?

LIZ: Please don't use that word at the table.

STAN: What word?

LIZ: Fuck. Don't say fuck at my table.

STAN: We know each other.

LIZ: You don't know me.

STAN: I know you.

LIZ: Tell me two things you think you know.

STAN: You hate the word "fuck" and you can't wait for Mike to come home.

LIZ: Okay. But I still think we could get to know each other.

(*The door slams open and like a gust of wind or a big storm,* TESSA *appears in the doorway, disheveled. She wears dark movie star glasses and perhaps a big coat. She looks like she's been through a storm or maybe Hell. CRASH*)

(STAN *and* LIZ *look up.*)

TESSA: Oh, fuck. (*Then, brightening for* STAN *and* LIZ) Hiya.

(*Pause.* STAN *and* LIZ *stare.*)

TESSA: Oh. Is this a bad time?

(*Blackout*)

(*Lights up*)

(STAN *and* LIZ *sit in their places as before.* TESSA *is not with them. Her stuff is though. And she has a lot of stuff.*)

LIZ: Is she staying long?

STAN: I don't know.

LIZ: Did you invite her?

STAN: I don't think so.

LIZ: You don't think so?

STAN: I mean, maybe.

LIZ: Maybe? Maybe? You said you *met* her. You said "met". You did not say "invite". You did not say you invited—

STAN: Well. I think maybe I vaguely remember saying like, "come anytime, we'd love to have you." But how many people do you say that to? A lot, right? You say it to a lot of people.

LIZ: I don't say it to a lot of people.

STAN: Sure you do. We do. We say, "Oh, we'd love to have you,"

LIZ: I don't know if we say that. I don't think I say that. Maybe you say that. But I don't think I say that. And if I do say that, usually they call and ask first. And usually they don't think you're serious. And, then, usually, even if they do decide to take you up on the, well not insincere, but certainly not sincerely motivated, offer, they at least bring a fruit basket. Deepak Chopra says that you're supposed to bring a gift whenever you visit someone's house. A basket of some sort.

STAN: Well, she sure as Hell isn't bringing any goddamn fruit basket.

LIZ: Exactly. Do you think she'll stay long?

STAN: I don't know.

LIZ: Because I am not spending the entire holiday season holding that woman's hand.

STAN: Of course not.

LIZ: I'm not.

STAN: I know.

LIZ: And you're not either.

(*And finally, back to* MIKE *and* JAMIE, *now off the bus and in the station.*)

MIKE: Who do you want to be in the new Millennium?

JAMIE: You ask a lot of questions.

MIKE: Who do you want to be?

JAMIE: I don't know.

MIKE: I do. I want to be kind. And fair. And adaptable. I want my parents to be proud of me. And I also want to be Luke Skywalker. Or God.

JAMIE: "Kind, fair and adaptable" aren't who. They're more like what.

MIKE: What?

JAMIE: "Kind, fair and adaptable" are qualities you want to have. Not people you want to be.

MIKE: Wow. You're right. Do you think I should change the question? Or just my answer?

JAMIE: You live outside the City?

MIKE: Yeah.

JAMIE: You come into the City?

MIKE: Probably.

JAMIE: I'll give you my number. At Candy's. Maybe we can have a beer.

MIKE: I don't really like beer. Can we have something else?

JAMIE: Whatever. Sure.

MIKE: Like, I don't know. Something.

JAMIE: We can have anything. So call me if the suburbs get to you.

MIKE: Does Candy know you're coming?

JAMIE: No.

MIKE: Yeah. You might need a friend. So who do you want to be?

JAMIE: Can I think about it and let you know?

MIKE: Yes. Yes, you can.

the magnitude of what is about to happen

(HOPE, *nineteen and a classmate of* MIKE'*s, is seen alone. She is very earnest.*)

HOPE: This is the story I am working on for class. It is about Loulou, a young woman who is in love with Bill, a young man who sits next to her in Fiction Writing One at a small almost Ivy college in upstate New York. He also, parenthetically, went to high school with her freshman roommate... whose name is Ivy. Ivy? I don't know. It might not fit in the story anyway. (Ivy might not fit in the story.)

Bill goes home to New York for the holidays. He takes a bus. From his college upstate. He takes a bus, and maybe he sits next to a stranger, a drifter. And they talk. They talk about love. The kind that makes you run from the room. The kind that takes over your heart and mind and makes everything else pale—

And Loulou, who is avoiding her home life altogether, spends her vacation with Ivy, the aforementioned freshman roommate, in New York City waiting and hoping to run into Bill. Casually. She will run into him casually at first, like they do in Jane Austen novels. And then, like Scott Fitzgerald and the beautiful, mad Zelda...okay, something about them, oh and there is a subplot involving key literary figures and research into socio-economic phenomena. The entire point of the subplot is to kick the main plot forward. This will provide the cue for Bill's entrance. But Bill misses his entrance, forcing Loulou into more direct action.

Loulou must seek out Bill. Directly.

(*She takes out the manuscript or page from her journal or whatever and reads...*)

Dear Bill. I'm coming to the City to find you. And if we are connected, and I know that we are, let me run into you at Grand Central Station or places people in New

York City go. I know about you. I pay attention. I feel
things. Everything all the time. I feel other peoples'
feelings. They flood me. But mostly I feel this. For you.
About you and for you.

Do you feel this, Bill? Do you understand the
magnitude of what is about to happen?

you won't even know i'm around

TESSA: You guys are so great to let me visit. I mean,
when you said, "Visit,", when you said, "Come
anytime," I thought, these are people who mean this.
Who really mean it. You wouldn't believe how many
people are just so full of shit. I mean, insincere. I mean,
they just say things. But you two, you're different. I
knew I could trust you right off.

STAN: Of course. You can trust us.

TESSA: Well, then I can tell you. I've disappeared.

LIZ: Disappeared how exactly?

TESSA: Well. I just left. I mean, sure, they could track
me down, my airline reservations, my goddamned
credit card, the F B I, you know the F B I is a real force.
But, no I just took off. Left and came here. I needed to
be with people I could trust. And this is good. Here.
So good. And I'll be good too. Quiet. You won't even
know I'm around.

STAN: We're glad you could come.

LIZ: Yes. We're very glad. And our son is coming home
soon. He's been at his first semester of college. These
are pictures of him.

(LIZ *shows* TESSA *pictures of* MIKE.)

LIZ: The pictures are from a long time ago when we
were a happy family. I mean, in the past.

STAN: Vassar. I think he's studying something like English. Something we really should pay a lot of money for him to study like it is not his native language.

TESSA: (*Pointing at a picture of* LIZ*)* Is this you?

STAN: So, it's really great that you're here.

LIZ: It's fine that you're here. For now.

TESSA: You won't even notice me. I'll just hole up in one of those guest rooms and be real quiet and good and—just read. I'll just read the whole time. Just 'til I get stronger. I'm kinda weak right now.

LIZ: Are you in some sort of trouble?

TESSA: Honey, I'm always in some sort of trouble. But I always get myself out. I'm pretty gifted that way.

homework = hold me

HOPE: "I am waiting for you to notice that I sit next to you in Fiction Writing One and that you can't live without me. We are the prince and princess of Western European countries in the nineteenth century, and our kingdoms need to merge. And once you fall in love with me, or merge, I would like for you to take me home for the holidays. Thanksgiving. Christmas. Whatever. So that I can avoid the people from my native land, the ones with my blood and genetic code information.

Do you know who I am? Did you know that that day I asked you about the homework I was secretly asking you to deflower me or least take me out for a coffee at The Retreat? You missed the secret code entirely. The part where 'Homework' translates to 'hold me'."

making friends

LIZ: I barely recognize him. He's huge. Enormous. And unrecognizable. Enormous and unrecognizable.

TESSA: He seems like a sweet kid. From those pictures.

LIZ: He's not a kid anymore. He's enormous.

TESSA: Yeah?

LIZ: Have you ever watched something grow like that?

TESSA: No.

LIZ: It's amazing.

TESSA: I bet.

LIZ: You don't have kids?

TESSA: No.

LIZ: It's really amazing. I can't wait to see him.

TESSA: Well, he seems like a sweet kid in the pictures. I like the one with the mittens. Do you all still have those mittens? You know the ones I mean? Do you save things? I do, I just save everything. The red ones in the pictures. He's holding up some kind of fish. And then he's like with a snowman. I mean I just about cried when I saw those sweet mittens on that sweet kid. That just about killed me. You know which ones I mean?

LIZ: I think so. The red ones. Are you staying through the holidays?

TESSA: What holidays?

LIZ: Chanukah, Christmas, New Years Eve and then New Years Day. The major ones. The ones coming next week.

TESSA: Um, I don't know. I'm having a crisis. Do you want me to go?

LIZ: What kind of a crisis?

TESSA: Do you want me to go?

LIZ: No. Of course not. What kind of a crisis?

TESSA: I ruin everyone. I don't want to ruin you or anything.

LIZ: Oh, I'm sure that's not true. I'm sure you don't ruin anyone.

TESSA: It is, though. I think it's my karma. I have really fucked up karma. And I'm having these nightmares about the French Revolution. It'd kinda help to not be alone right now.

LIZ: I'm sure you don't ruin everyone.

TESSA: I do. I'm like Whatshername.

LIZ: What's her name?

TESSA: You know. The Indian.

LIZ: Pocahontas?

TESSA: No, the *Indian*. Like from India. That kind of Indian. The one that's...like...she's got these really big teeth. You know who I mean? She destroys everything but they love her anyway. And they have all these holidays just for her. Do you know who I mean? 'Cause I think if I'm gonna be destructive, I could at least be like that.

LIZ: I don't know who you mean.

TESSA: I don't have a lot of friends, Liz.

LIZ: Well it must be very hard. In your line of work. I mean, you don't trust many people. You can't. But we should try to be friends. Lets just, you and me, find some common ground. You see, I do have women friends. I love women.

TESSA: You think I don't love women?

LIZ: I didn't say that.

TESSA: You just said I don't love women.

LIZ: No, I said that—I mean, I think I said—I don't know what I said.

TESSA: Cause I think you're the one who doesn't trust. You can't in your line of work, either. Can you?

don't you want me, baby?

HOPE: It's a bad song, the way I feel about you, Bill, I mean Mike. It's a Human League song from the 1980's. The Human League was a band. They did songs like "Don't you Want Me Baby" and "The Things That Dreams Are Made Of." I am taking a class called "The Split Culture of the Nineteen Eighties" at Vassar this term. We listen to lots of music like Human League and Soft Cell and Flock of Seagulls. Thomas Dolby, too. "Europa and the Pirate Twins" This was a movement called "New Wave". I think it was very important and connected to a sort of neoromantic impulse in a Cold War culture. It was totally different than punk rock. And in this class, we look at the variations in youth culture (Punk versus New Wave for instance) and the revolt away from the dominant culture's materialistic Reagan values. It's a fascinating class because you think you know something about a time because it was recent. Like, just twenty years ago recent. But then you study it like it's history, and you learn all about what it *really* was. You put it into a context. And it says something too about where we are now. On the edge of the 21st century.

I want to be a writer. I'm collecting peoples' stories. To do something with. To write about. But mostly, I am collecting my own. I have a lot of my own stories. I am fairly bursting over with them. And I have many unsent letters. To Mike.

Did I tell you about Mike? He sits next to me in

Fiction One. He's from New York. He says things. I like him.

home

(MIKE *lets himself into the house. No one is there to greet him.*)

MIKE: Who do you want to be in the new Millennium? Well...I think basically I want everything to shatter and break apart. No, I'm just kidding.
  Welcome home.

(TESSA *on a cell phone in the living room. In a secret lover whisper.*)

TESSA: Hey, it's me. I'm here. I'm here, and it's me. Yeah. My friends here are wonderful. Oh, they really care about me. I mean, I just met them and they opened their home to me and they were thrilled about it. You can tell they really want me here. For the Holidays. Like I'm part of the fucking family. What? I sound needy? Fuck you. If I'm needy, it's for a good reason. Yeah I know, "larger things are at stake." Fuck you. Fuck you and kiss my ass.
(*She hangs up on her caller. Goes to the bar*)
There is a fine line between movie star and whore.
(*She pours herself a drink.*)
It is time to be wildly happy. Time for us to be the good guys, the ones in the white hats. I need some good guys in my life. Some real good guys. They're kinda hard to find. But I'm gonna be one. I'm gonna find one, and I'm gonna be one. In a big white hat.

MIKE: Uh. Hi.

TESSA: Hi yourself.

MIKE: I'm Mike. I live here.

TESSA: Oh, yeah? The little boy with the mittens.

MIKE: (*He has no idea what she's talking about.*) Stan and Liz's son.

TESSA: Yeah? I'm Tessa.

MIKE: I know who you are. What are you doing in my house? Do you know my mom and dad? They've never mentioned you. I mean, you'd think they'd mention someone like you.

TESSA: Met your dad in the City. At a big party. You like big parties?

MIKE: Sure. I mean, I don't go to many. We've had a few at school. Not many though. Probably not like the kind you go to. I bet you go to lots of parties. Do you know where my parents are?

TESSA: You're cute.

MIKE: What are you doing here? I mean, what are you doing here?

TESSA: (*Shakes her head yes*) Staying. Is that okay?

MIKE: Wow. Yeah. Of course it's okay. But, I mean, how come? Like couldn't you just stay with some millionaire or something? You don't have to answer that. I ask too many questions. My dad would kill me if he knew I was bothering you.

TESSA: No, it's okay. See, it's like this...

(MIKE *settles down to listen.*)

TESSA: Something happened to me. And I can't tell you what exactly, but it doesn't matter cause it was a whole lot of things rolled into one, and when the one came about, it was like I saw something. It was one of those moments people talk about. What they call a watershed. like a bad thing happens and then you have one of these watersheds. And I've been feeling everything in a new way. Only I don't exactly know what to do about it yet. So I had to go somewhere and figure stuff out. And I didn't want to be alone. See, I can't be alone right now. It's bad when I'm alone. I don't sleep. Do you sleep?

MIKE: I sleep okay. Do you want to talk about the watershed? I mean you can tell me. I'm a writer.

TESSA: You don't say.

MIKE: Yeah. I do say. I'm going to be a writer.

TESSA: I saw your picture.

MIKE: You did?

TESSA: A little boy with mittens on the front of Christmas card. That's you?

MIKE: Yeah. That's me.

TESSA: No. That was a little boy with mittens. You're a man.

MIKE: Yeah?

TESSA: Enormous and unrecognizable. Hey, you want a Martini, Enormous and Unrecognizable Mike?

MIKE: Sure.

TESSA: Great. 'Cause I hate to drink alone. *(She starts to make them Martinis.)* Is that short for, what, Michael? Mitchell? Is it short for something, Mike?

MIKE: Michael.

TESSA: Yeah? What else?

MIKE: Michael Anton.

TESSA: Anton, eh?

MIKE: Yeah.

TESSA: You're going to be a heartbreaker, you know.

MIKE: You think?

TESSA: Oh, yeah.

MIKE: I'm going to be a writer.

TESSA: You told me.

MIKE: So, I'm collecting stories. I mean, you could tell me yours.

TESSA: I don't think you'd like my stories.

MIKE: Oh, I'm sure I would.

TESSA: I'll think about it. I have enough of 'em.

MIKE: You do? I don't have any. That's why I need to hear other peoples. I need a story of my own.

TESSA: You have a story. You just don't know what it is yet.

(TESSA *clinks glasses with* MIKE.)

TESSA: To love and happiness.

(MIKE *and* TESSA *drink.*)

(STAN *enters.* MIKE *jumps, tries to hide the martini glass immediately or backs away from it.*)

STAN: Well.

TESSA: Look who's here.

STAN: Michael.

TESSA: No, I know he's here. I meant you. You're here.

STAN: When did you get in?

MIKE: Just now.

STAN: Good. Glad to see you. Good. How was school? Want a...something? Juice something?

MIKE: No, thank you. I had some coffee when I got off the bus. I'm still reeling from that coffee. It wiped me out, you know. I can't take caffeine. It really wiped me out.

TESSA: Mike here, with the mittens, shouldn't drink coffee. Coffee messes me up too. Gin doesn't mess me up.

STAN: Clearly. (*Then to* MIKE*)* Your mother went to go... do something. I don't know. (*Beat*) Well. Glad you're home.

MIKE: Thanks, Dad.

STAN: Okay.

(*This is a very awkward moment.*)

TESSA: Who wants a drink?

bad nerves

STAN: Don't bother Tessa.

MIKE: Fine.

STAN: She's here to rest her nerves. She has bad nerves. And I'm sure she hates people bothering her all the time. I bet they bother her all the time.

MIKE: Fine.

STAN: So, don't.

MIKE: Okay.

STAN: And don't stare.

MIKE: Fine.

STAN: Fine what?

MIKE: Fine, Dad. I won't stare.

STAN: Good.

MIKE: Fine.

STAN: How's school?

MIKE: It's fine.

STAN: You...like your classes?

MIKE: Yes.

STAN: Okay. Well. Glad to have you home.

more bad nerves

STAN: I'm sorry if he was bothering you.

TESSA: He wasn't bothering me.

STAN: Can I get you anything?

TESSA: Like what?

STAN: I don't know. What do you need?

TESSA: Lots. I need lots.

STAN: Oh. Well. If there's anything I can do— If you need certain kinds of food, or if you want to go somewhere, if you need a ride, I mean, I don't know, what kinds of things do you need?

TESSA: I need really big things right now. But we can start small, you and me.

aria(s)

LIZ: Each room in the house has a theme. That's the key to good decorating. Working with a theme. This one, for instance. This room has a Colonial theme. It's Colonial. Note the powder blue walls and the lace. One day, when Mike was about seven, he went around and named each of the rooms in the house. He called this one Agnes.

Mike did lots of things.

Liz did lots of things.

Stan did lots of things.

Everyone did lots of things. Lots of things were done. We all did them. We did many things and many things were done. Lots, in fact. Just lots.

Liz has a secret. Will Liz tell her secret? Will Liz die trying? Will Liz escape to the other side? Is there another side? Will Liz leave Stan? Will Stan leave

Liz? Will they work on the marriage like the marriage
counselor said to? Will they start to make treasure
maps of one another's bodies? Will they find hidden
treasure. Tune in. This and More. Next week. Tune in
next week. Tune in, turn on... Don't drop out. Don't fall. Don't go. Don't drop. Don't
do that. Don't say that to your father.
Do wash your face. Do brush your teeth. Do take that
SAT class, I think it's a good thing. Don't worry if that
girl doesn't call you back. She doesn't understand how
wonderful you are, and that is her loss and not yours.
Do make sure you're home by midnight. Please? Don't
worry if you can't finish everything on your plate.
It's stupid anyway, that thing about starving kids
somewhere. They don't care either way what you do
with your plate —they just want to get fed.

How will they get fed?

TESSA: Okay, this is the dream I keep having. It's the
French revolution, and I'm up on this big platform, like
a prisoner. I'm up on this kind of chopping block in
front of a whole crowd of people. And there are other
people I know up there with me. Like prisoners. And
there's this man in a black hood— And up until now,
it's all been kinda okay, like nothing's been real—but
then it gets real, it gets very, very real. And there's
blood everywhere. Blood and people's heads. There
are heads. It's some kind of massacre. And then I get
it: they're gonna kill me. And it's true. They are. And
just before the moment of impact, my soul freezes
up. It just freezes. And I'm thinking, "How could
this happen?" Cause it's really happening; this guy's
cutting my head off. Cause before this, I don't know,
maybe I thought they were bluffing. But they are not
bluffing. And the blade comes down and just touches
my neck, and that's when I wake up. Horrified and like
I can't breathe. And the thing is, they were right to cut

my head off. I was a terrible person. They were hungry and I didn't care. (*She fingers her neck.*)

STAN: Did anyone else care? Because, I'm thinking you can only be as good as your general surroundings.

TESSA: That sounds kinda fucked to me. The point was I was like this terrible person. You want to make me another drink? It's time for another goddamned martini.

(HOPE *by candlelight. At night:*)

HOPE: My roommate Antoinette says I think too much. She says, I used to think that much, and I had to stop. She says, "You think about everything, and then you think about it again."
Yeah, so?
I mean, this is not a problem. Thinking is not a problem. Digesting is not a problem. None of these things are problems. I know what I want. What others call "idealism" —it just means I have vision. I know what I want. And what to create. Duh.

in the middle of the night...

(TESSA *is sitting in the dark eating ice cream out of the carton. There is something unkempt about her.* MIKE *enters and turns on the lights, startling her.*)

MIKE/TESSA: Oh!

MIKE: Oh. Sorry. I didn't mean to scare you. —Should I go?

TESSA: No, no, no —you stay. It's fine. I'm fine.

MIKE: What are you doing? Eating?

TESSA: Looks that way.

MIKE: Can I join you? (*He does, pulling up a chair.*) Who do you want to be in the new Millennium?

TESSA: What?

MIKE: Who do you want to be?

TESSA: Is it a trick question?

MIKE: No.

TESSA: Can I be me?

MIKE: Sure.

TESSA: Who do you want to be?

MIKE: Luke Skywalker.

TESSA: Yeah? Like in the movie?

MIKE: Yeah.

TESSA: Who do I want to be? I've never wanted to be anyone else.

MIKE: See, because it's a whole new thing.

TESSA: I want to be wildly happy. Can I be that?

MIKE: No. That isn't a who. It's a what.

TESSA: It's a what?

MIKE: Yeah. Exactly. It isn't a who.

TESSA: I don't get you.

MIKE: Wildly happy isn't a who, it's a what.

TESSA: Oh. (*She looks at him like "You're fucking adorable".*)

MIKE: But you could be a who.

TESSA: I see.

MIKE: You see? What do you see?

(MIKE *and* TESSA *share a moment. It is genuine.*)

TESSA: I see something nice about you. About who you might be someday.

MIKE: Yeah?

TESSA: Yeah.

(MIKE *and* TESSA *share a moment.*)

TESSA: Tell me about this college of yours.

MIKE: What about it?

TESSA: What's it like?

MIKE: Um. Well. It's good. I mean, it's my first semester. But it's good. Did you go to college?

TESSA: No. I got into other things. I wanted to be an actress. In the movies. But not just an actress. I wanted to be, like, a Being.

MIKE: Yeah. It's hard to be a Being in college. You have to do all this other stuff.

TESSA: Yeah, you always got to do the other stuff, huh? Sometimes I think about it though. I know a lot about how the world works. Street smart. But sometimes...I wish I knew other things. You gotta know all sorts of things when you go to college. About like...Dickens, right? And...that other one. *Moby Dick.* I wish I knew about Dickens and Moby Dick.

MIKE: Melville.

TESSA: Sure. Like that.

MIKE: Melville wrote *Moby Dick.* Dickens wrote... a lot of other stuff. Big long stories. *A Tale of Two Cities* is about the French Revolution.

TESSA: Yeah? I was in the French Revolution. I was a really bad person.

MIKE: I'm sorry if I'm embarrassing you, but you are the most beautiful woman I have ever seen. Ever in my entire life. Oh, God, I can't believe I said that. But do you even know how totally perfect and beautiful you are?

TESSA: 'Kay, that's enough. What about you?

MIKE: What about me what?

TESSA: What do you want out of life?

MIKE: I don't think I know yet. But I met this guy on the bus and he talked all about this kind of dangerous love, and that sounded pretty good to me.

TESSA: I know about dangerous love. That is one thing I know.

MIKE: You do?

TESSA: It's kinda one of my specialties.

(MIKE *and* TESSA*'s eyes lock. Oh, my. They breathe at the same time.*)

MIKE: See? That is just so perfect. Because you're here. At my parents house. And you know all about the thing I want to know about. This is called synchronicity.

TESSA: Let's trade. I teach you about dangerous love, and you teach me about...Dickens.

MIKE: Charles.

TESSA: Hmm?

MIKE: His name was Charles. Charles Dickens.

TESSA: Oh yeah? Great. And tell me each of the things he wrote.

MIKE: Okay.

(*With each of the titles,* TESSA *gives* MIKE *something. If it's a kiss, it is a tiny kiss. This should be very erotic.*)

MIKE: A Tale of Two Cities.

TESSA: Uh-huh.

MIKE: Oliver Twist.

TESSA: Great

MIKE: Um, Little Dorrit?

TESSA: (*No, that can't be it/don't shit me*) Come on.

MIKE: Come on what?

TESSA: That isn't what it's called.

MIKE: (*Winning back her touch*) Yes. It is. And...um...oh, yeah, *A Christmas Carol*. You know. The one with Tiny Tim and Scrooge. Everyone knows that one.

TESSA: (*Back in the game*) Sure. I love that one.

MIKE: *Pickwick Papers* (1836-37); *Oliver Twist* (1837-39); *Nicholas Nickleby* (1838-39); *The Old Curiosity Shop* (1840-41); *Barnaby Rudge* (1841); *Martin Chuzzlewit* (1843-44); *Dombey and Son* (1846-48); *David Copperfield* (1849-50); *Bleak House* (1852- 53); *Hard Times* (1854); *Little Dorrit* (1855-57); *A Tale of Two Cities* (1859); *Great Expectations* (1860-61); *Our Mutual Friend* (1864-65); *Edwin Drood* (unfinished, 1870)

(MIKE *and* TESSA *come very near to kissing. They both want to. They get very, very near to it. She pulls away.*)

TESSA: Okay, let's stop there. For tonight.

MIKE: I could give you homework. Something to read. I mean, I have all these books. In my room.

TESSA: I think we should give it a rest. Just for now.

MIKE: But I have all these books in my room. You wanna see my room? I have all sorts of cool stuff up there. Books and C Ds and Playstation...all kinds of stuff.

TESSA: I can't.

MIKE: How come?

(TESSA *kisses* MIKE.)

TESSA: That's how come. I could get into trouble with you. You're just so goddamned sweet.

MIKE: Get into trouble.

TESSA: I gotta be good.

MIKE: Don't be good.

TESSA: But I gotta be. It's the new millennium. Remember?

MIKE: Not 'til next week.

TESSA: Still. Not tonight, Michael Anton. Maybe another time. After I know all about Charles Dickens and that other guy.

MIKE: Melville.

TESSA: Yeah, him.

i'm gonna love you too

HOPE: So, I was thinking, maybe we could, um get together while we're on break ... I'm going to be going up to that town you live in. Where do you live again? Westchester? That's in the suburbs, right? I could just take the Metro North and come up there.

I know you think I'm a stalker. But I'm not a stalker. I'm just a girl. And this is what girls do sometimes. We write letters and send email and leave messages and check our caller I D and hang up before you answer. Sometimes this is what girls have to do.

liquid and fluid

(*Lights up on* JAMIE *outside Candy's apartment somewhere in Chinatown.*)

JAMIE: Keeping things liquid and fluid. Liquid. And fluid too. I'm here, I'm here, I'm standing right here, turn around and see me, Candy. See me and invite me upstairs, and out of the goddamn rain.

the next morning.

(TESSA *sits on the lawn, wrapped in fur, smoking a cigarette and wearing dark glasses and some sort of scarf as if in disguise.* HOPE *approaches cautiously.*)

TESSA: Michael Anton, eh? Michael Anton, I gotta get your sweet face back underneath my hands.

HOPE: Hello.

TESSA: Hi, there.

HOPE: Is this, am I in the right place?

TESSA: I don't know, Honey. What place is right?

HOPE: Well. I'm looking for Mike. He sits next to me in Fiction One.

TESSA: Does he?

HOPE: Yes. He does. And I'm going to be a writer. And I'm here to get Mike and take him with me.

TESSA: Really? How interesting.

HOPE: Yes. So, is this the wrong place? Or the right place?

TESSA: I think it's the right place. The rightest place. What's your name, Honey?

HOPE: Hope.

TESSA: Hope? Perfect.

(*Blackout*)

END OF ACT ONE

"your understanding about transition, death, loss and separation will be important at this time—for there will be those who accompany you and those who do not."
—*Sunlight on Water*

ACT TWO

the new world

(Lights up on LIZ, TESSA *and* HOPE.*)*

LIZ: I'm a little confused. I mean, I love meeting Mike's friends, and friends from college certainly, but I can't quite place you. Were you there at Parents Weekend?

HOPE: I sit next to Mike. I'm a writer. I don't think we met at Parents Weekend.

LIZ: I see.

HOPE: And I was in the neighborhood.

LIZ: Really?

HOPE: Well, I was on the Metro North. And then I got off. And I was in the neighborhood.

LIZ: I see.

HOPE: Yes. My roommate from Vassar—

TESSA: Antoinette.

HOPE: —went to Riverdale with Mike, and I was staying with her over the holidays, but she's gone away for the weekend, and I was in her apartment, and um, well, I just took this train ride here, and kind of...

TESSA: It's okay, Honey. You don't have to tell her everything.

HOPE: My mom gets tired a lot. She has chronic fatigue.

TESSA: I said you don't have to tell her everything.

HOPE: Well, I don't know. She hasn't been to a doctor. But I think she must have chronic fatigue because she is always tired. Chronically fatigued and tired. And she sleeps a lot.

TESSA: Sounds like depression to me.

LIZ: Well. I mean, that would be fine. You're a friend of Mike's from school. Of course you can stay. The weekend. You can spend the weekend.

HOPE: Are you sure it's okay?

LIZ: Of course it's okay.

HOPE: Thank you.

LIZ: You're far from home. Where's home again?

HOPE: Far.

LIZ: I see.

TESSA: I think it's a great idea.

LIZ: It is a great idea. And, it'll give Mike someone to talk to. A peer.

real magic

(MIKE *and* TESSA *engaged in one of their "lessons".*)

MIKE: Listen. I wrote this.
"Like fake magic, her laugh
Blazing copper fire, her hair..."
What do you think? It's just the first two lines. That's all I have. But, I mean, what do you think?

TESSA: It's okay.

MIKE: Yeah?

TESSA: Why fake magic? Why not real magic?

MIKE: I don't know. Do you like it?

TESSA: I just think the magic should be real.

MIKE: Well, it is real, but in the poem, it's fake.

TESSA: That's stupid.

MIKE: You don't like it?

TESSA: I don't know.

MIKE: Oh. (*Crushed*) Why is it that human beings aren't covered in fur? Don't you think it's kind of interesting that we have skin and not fur?

TESSA: No.

MIKE: Why do we have skin?

TESSA: Oh, Jesus, Kid, you're giving me a headache.

MIKE: But I want to know. I really want to know.

TESSA: This is why we have skin.

(TESSA *touches* MIKE. *This is erotic. She then goes back to what she's doing. Knitting? Reading?*)

MIKE: Oh. That's a good reason.

TESSA: Tell me about the girl.

MIKE: What girl?

TESSA: With the notebooks.

MIKE: Hope?

TESSA: Yeah. Hope.

MIKE: What about her?

TESSA: I don't know. Who is she?

MIKE: I don't know really. I don't know her all that well. She's...well, she's Hope, and she...I think she sits next to me in a class. I'm not sure which one. Someone she knows knows me. So, I know her in that way. Through people. I'm not really clear exactly on what she's doing here. But I mean, things like that happen all the time when you're a writer. Girls and unexpected people show up during the break between semesters. I think I want to live my whole life this way. Just being open. To anyone who shows up. Unexpected houseguests. Like you. You're so unexpected.

TESSA: Just to you. I'm not unexpected to me.

MIKE: I know. And I'm glad. That you're here.

TESSA: You're just saying that cuz I kissed you.

MIKE: Maybe.

TESSA: Yeah.

MIKE: Maybe.

TESSA: And we're not telling anyone. Right?

MIKE: Right.

TESSA: I like her.

MIKE: Who?

TESSA: The girl.

MIKE: Hope?

TESSA: Yeah. Hope. Something about her, I like.

MIKE: Would you stop talking about Hope?

TESSA: She likes you.

MIKE: You think?

TESSA: Oh yeah. What are we reading today?

MIKE: Oliver Twist.

TESSA: Yeah? He was an orphan, right? Like me. I know all about that orphan stuff.

MIKE: I want to be good to you. In all sorts of ways. I want to be there and help you through this watershed moment and be your friend and listen to you and write poems about your hair, and kiss you and take care of you. I mean, I could take care of you. Kind of.

TESSA: You want to take care of me?

MIKE: I want to kiss you again. Can I?

TESSA: No. Yeah, okay.

(*She kisses him. It's intense. Hungry and sweet at the same time.*)

TESSA: Spend time with her.

MIKE: Who?

TESSA: Hope.

MIKE: Yeah, okay. Hope —

(MIKE *pulls* TESSA*'s mouth back to his. They kiss again.*)

fight with me

LIZ: Fight with me.

STAN: What are you talking about?

LIZ: I want you to fight with me.

STAN: What do you want to fight about?

LIZ: I don't care. I think we need to fight.

STAN: We don't need to fight.

LIZ: We have a problem.

STAN: We don't have a problem.

LIZ: We don't have a problem?

STAN: We're fine. You are making these problems up, and frankly, it makes me tired.

LIZ: I see.

STAN: Can we just have lunch and be happy? We're fine.

LIZ: We're not fine.

STAN: I'm fine.

LIZ: Okay. We're fine.

(Lights change as LIZ *addresses the audience. An aria)*

LIZ: I took Tessa shopping. She wasn't wearing underwear. Normally that would be fine. I mean it is certainly none of my business. Everyone can make their own decisions about that sort of thing. But you cannot try on pants at Barney's without something underneath. That's why they call them under-pants. You have to wear them under pants, under the pants you are thinking of purchasing, or not, when you are trying things on at expensive department stores. It's a rule. The law, maybe. Especially if you are the type to leave stains. Which, I gather, she is. So we had to send Monique or whoever upstairs to lingerie on five to buy Tessa a pair of Calvin Klein underpants. And it was a success. She bought a coat.

liberal arts

TESSA: Okay. What do they teach you at this school? Vassar.

HOPE: Lots of things. Liberal Arts. Deconstruction and postmodernism. Poetry. Foundations of western culture. The Greeks. You know.

TESSA: That's what I was afraid of. We have to start at the beginning. Take notes.

*(*HOPE *gets her notebook.)*

TESSA: First thing: Nobody else can make you happy. Nobody can make you anything. They just, like, give you what you already are. They kinda reflect it back. Next thing: There are two kind of people -- the kind who wear the magic and the kind who swallow it. And you want to wear it. You see what I'm getting at?

HOPE: Kind of.

TESSA: Good. Any questions?

HOPE: Yes. Just one. Do you have any regrets?

TESSA: No.

HOPE: Wow.

TESSA: Yeah. (*This is NOT sentimental*) Okay, some. I regret not having a kid. And I regret not telling more people to fuck off. I'm sorry I let them boss me around. I'm sorry that love didn't last. Not just romance. You expect romance not to last. But love's s'posed to. Things change. People turn. People who loved you stop. People think you're a bitch. (*She looks at* HOPE) Okay, maybe they won't think *you're* a bitch. But me, they think I'm a bitch. You think it's worth it?

HOPE: Worth what?

TESSA: The whole thing, Honey. All of it.

HOPE: Fame?

TESSA: Life. Life takes a lot out of a girl. It kicks my ass again and again. I mean, being alive is great. But life kicks my ass.

HOPE: Do you think we need a new world?

TESSA: You bet we do.

HOPE: Would you like to come be in it with me? I'm going to be in it, and you could join me if you like. It might be just what you need.

TESSA: That's real sweet, Honey. But I'm kinda locked into this one.

HOPE: This one is a dead end.

TESSA: You're right about that.

HOPE: It's just not working. Everyone's falling apart and pretending not to. And they all go on like usual and take more anti-depressants and drink and buy stuff they don't need and act really clever and cynical, but really, really they just need to jump ship. Did you see *Titanic*?

TESSA: I saw *Poseidon Adventure*.

HOPE: We have to jump ship. You could be a mom in the new world.

TESSA: I'd be a shitty mom.

HOPE: No, you'd be great. I know you would.

TESSA: Look at me. I make the same mistakes over and over.

HOPE: Well, that's what I'm getting at. You don't have to make those mistakes. Everything could be different.

TESSA: Like what?

HOPE: Everything. The very foundations.

TESSA: You have strong feelings about this.

HOPE: Oh yes. It's kind of a passion with me. Not a hobby. Not a phase. A passion.

TESSA: Yeah? I guess that's kind of a good thing. Idealism.

HOPE: No. It is more than idealism. It is a new way.

TESSA: Yeah? What kind of new way?

HOPE: A completely new way. New in all new ways. I can't tell you more than that. It has to be experienced and not described. I'll be your kid. If you want. I mean, you could be a mother because I could be your kid.

TESSA: Honey, I think you already are.

singing it into being

MIKE: I think it's great how you're traveling around right now.

HOPE: How I'm what?

MIKE: I met this guy on the bus and he was traveling around.

HOPE: I'm not traveling around.

MIKE: Oh.

HOPE: I want to start a new world.

MIKE: Really?

HOPE: Yes. What do you think about that?

MIKE: Well. I don't know. What's wrong with the world you're in?

HOPE: It leaves me wanting.

MIKE: It leaves you wanting what?

HOPE: Everything. Don't you feel that? Like something's missing.

MIKE: A lot's missing.

HOPE: Exactly. The very foundations are crumbling. Falling by the wayside and people hunger for something more.

MIKE: They do.

HOPE: They do. For example, Vassar—

MIKE: Vassar?

HOPE: It is a wondrous thing to be at Vassar College, where Edna Saint Vincent Millay and tons of other extraordinary people went to school, instead of SUNY Albany which has better financial aid packages, and yet at this wondrous place, why are so many mean people unaware of the very wondrousness of it and also, why are they taking up space, filling the air with their very meanness? It is time to overthrow.

MIKE: Is this a political statement?

HOPE: It is a metaphysical statement. But it is also political. And psychological. And spiritual. And economic. And erotic, that means sexy. I think that it is a foundational shift away from one set of beliefs and towards another. And I don't know a lot about what the new one is, but I feel it inside of me. You can have what you really want. You can create the world anew. Sing it into being. Like the Aborigines.

MIKE: The Aborigines?

HOPE: I'm reading this book about them. They sing the world into being.

MIKE: Really?

HOPE: Yes. We can shape the world. Not only *can* we— but we have to. It's what we're here for. What if you could fulfill your larger self?

MIKE: I don't know.

HOPE: Well, I intend to. Fulfill my larger self. I can. I'm very strong.

MIKE: I see that.

HOPE: So what do you think? Would you like to come with me? And fulfill your larger self?

MIKE: Well...

HOPE: Your very soul is hungering for it. And the new world needs you. We can sing it into being. And you have so much to contribute.

MIKE: I do? Like what?

HOPE: Well. Yourself. You could contribute your self *(She faces the audience for her aria.)* You could love me. That's what. And that would be enough. That would be wonderful. Just like in the Blondie song. Like in my class on the mixed culture. You could love me and I could love you too. "You're gonna tell me sweet things, you're gonna make my heart sing, and you're gonna say you love me, and I'm gonna love you too." Because that is how I feel about you. This time, this place, this year. Larchmont, New York on the cusp between worlds. I'm going to. And I do. I do.

(Blondie song I'm Gonna Love You Too *comes up VERY LOUD.* HOPE *dances.)*

scoring

*(*TESSA *and* MIKE *are in their underwear playing games on Playstation—)*

TESSA: You're karate chopping my ass, Kid—

MIKE: No, you're just new. You're not used to the—

TESSA: Darling. I am so used to the—joystick?

MIKE: That's not what it's called anymore. Look. Use it—exactly—like that—see, and you can shoot lasers—

TESSA: I like lasers.

MIKE: Yes. Oh. Your lifeline's disappearing.

TESSA: Fuck.

MIKE: I'm sorry. You have to try again. Come on—

TESSA: It's time.

MIKE: *(Still locked on Playstation)* For what?

TESSA: Come here.

MIKE: Now?

TESSA: Now. *(Beat)* This is the best part. My favorite part. When you haven't yet. But you know you will. And it's so close.... This is my favorite part.

(MIKE *and* TESSA *breathe together.*)

TESSA: But, it's part of the trade, okay? Then you go back to being a sweet kid, and I go back to grown ups. Got it?

MIKE: It's just part of the trade.

TESSA: Exactly.

MIKE: But what if it's something else?

TESSA: What else could it be, Michael Anton? I mean, what else could it be?

(MIKE *and* TESSA *start to make love. Then he turns to the audience for his aria.*)

MIKE: Semester break is the break between semesters. Which happens to correspond with the major holidays of Christmas, sometimes Chanukah and always New Years. But it isn't about the holidays, per se, so much as about the break itself. I like Chinatown. I used to go a bar there when I was in high school. The Triple Happiness. I liked the name. I like words. I like you. I like you a lot. I like the way you smell. Alcohol and perfume. I don't drink alcohol. I don't wear perfume. But you do. You drink and you smell good. I like you. I do not like being who I have to be sometimes. I wish I could be someone else. Someone older. Someone in a war. Someone on the frontlines. Someone brave. Someone you could love and respect and not some kid with red mittens holding up a fish.

hope in the garden

HOPE: I am not a wildflower. You think I'm boring, but I'm not boring. I want to find myself alone with you. In a garden. I want to take you to a garden. And I want you to take me to all the places you go, to get a tattoo, and—

(STAN *enters.*)

STAN: You can't do that here. You can't talk to the garden. This is Westchester, and people will think you're on drugs.

HOPE: I'm a friend of Mike's from Vassar. I'm not on drugs. Do you believe in the possibility of a totally new world within our lifetime?

STAN: I don't understand the question.

HOPE: Well. If things could change –

STAN: Change how?

HOPE: What if you could be who you really are?

STAN: A lot would change

HOPE: Do you want that?

STAN: Sure.

HOPE: You do?

STAN: Yes. But, we have jobs. It's hard to believe in a totally new world within our lifetime when you have a job.

(HOPE *looks at* STAN, *clearly disappointed.*)

HOPE: I have to go inside now. I'm cold. (*She goes into the house.*)

(STAN *turns to the audience for* his *aria.*)

STAN: Michael was her idea. I would have called him Zeke. Zeke'd be my kid. And he would not go to Vassar College. No. My Zeke would get out of

high school and hitch-hike across the country with
a messy girl named Sally. She's a mess, that Sally.
Like Tessa, only her name is Sally, and she's not so...
big. And Zeke'd be such a goddamned hard working
entrepreneurial son of a bitch. It wouldn't matter
whether he'd gone to college or studied English. Hell,
Zeke wouldn't need English. He'd make his own
language. And I want to be Zeke, and end up in Vegas
with someone warm like Sally. But you can't be Zeke
when you have to pay for everyone and drive them
home. And your son's name is Michael. And Sally
doesn't even know you're alive.

sloppy drunk

(STAN *and* TESSA *are both drinking martinis*)

TESSA: I don't know if I can be one of the guys with the
white hats. What if I'm not set up that way?

STAN: What the fuck are you talking about?

TESSA: The guys with the white hats, Stan. I don't think
I'm one of 'em. I tried. But I'm just not. I'm more like
that bitch with the big teeth.

STAN: You're a sloppy drunk.

TESSA: I am not.

STAN: You think I don't feel things? I do. I feel things.

TESSA: I think you're a sloppy drunk.

STAN: Kiss me.

TESSA: No. That would be wrong. Even for me.

not a wild flower

Liz: You think I'm boring. A housewife. A mother. A woman who does not leave stains. Not a wildflower. Not like you. I have gardeners. They arrive on Tuesdays and Thursdays and they trim all my overgrowth and take out the weeds and they clip anything unruly. I was planned and thought out. I look good in little suits. And you know nothing about me. There's more to it than meets the eye. And I want it to meet your eye. I want all the things you don't know about me to meet your eye and stay. I want to find myself alone with you again. In a fitting room at Barney's looking at your tattoos. Or somewhere else altogether. A garden. Or the shore. Would you go to the shore with me? Just the two of us? Because you're right. I don't have many friends in my line of work. But I think my line of work could change.

writing

Hope: Mike did lots of things. Liz did lots of things. Mike is enormous. A son, the sun, Mike is Apollo and he draws the chariot across the sky every day. And I want it to meet your eye, meet your eye and stay. I want to get your sweet face back underneath my—

(Mike *enters.*)

Mike: Uh... Hi.

Hope: Hi.

Mike: What are you doing?

Hope: Nothing. Writing. Have you thought about what I said?

Mike: What did you say?

Hope: You know. Singing.

MIKE: Oh. I don't know about that. I don't know.

HOPE: What don't you know?

MIKE: What do you think about skin? Why do you think we have it and not fur?

HOPE: I don't know. What is it you don't know? Please answer this question.

MIKE: I don't know. All of it. Reality. Life. Do you think maybe you should get a grip?

HOPE: A grip on what? What is there to get a grip on?

MIKE: I don't know.

HOPE: Oh, and you have this grip?

MIKE: I don't know.

HOPE: There is nothing here to grip on to. That's why we need to start fresh. What kind of grip am I supposed to get?

MIKE: I don't know.

HOPE: You either want this or you don't.

MIKE: Want what?

HOPE: Everything old to shatter and break apart. For us.

MIKE: Us?

HOPE: Well, yes.

MIKE: I don't know.

HOPE: Maybe you need time. I have that. I have the whole weekend and I can wait. I'll wait (*She exits.*)

cacophony of conflict

(TESSA *appears, disheveled and wrapped in a towel or terry cloth robe. Her hair is wet. This whole scene happens at a peak—*)

TESSA: Can you overdose on champagne and Excedrin for Migraines? That's all you have in the house. I mean, Excedrin for Migraines?

LIZ: You didn't overdose, Tessa. You're still here.

TESSA: Well, whose fucking fault was that? Excedrin for Migraines!?

STAN: Okay. I think you've been here long enough. I don' know what about our invitation made it sound sincere, but it wasn't. Okay? We are not sincere people.

LIZ: We are. We are sincere. I'm sincere. We were surprised, frankly—but you stay as long as you like. We want you here.

TESSA: I don't want to end up alone, Liz.

LIZ: You won't. I promise you. You just won't.

TESSA: I don't want to be like Garbo.

STAN: You're hardly Garbo.

TESSA: (*A different tone altogether*) Fuck you.

STAN: Well. You are not like Garbo. You are nothing like Garbo.

LIZ: Tessa, you won't end up alone. Because you don't want to. that's all. And I think Garbo was happy. I think she was happy alone.

(MIKE *enters.*)

MIKE: Tessa? I love you. I do. I love you. You don't have to love me back. But I love you and I have to say it out loud.

(HOPE *enters.*)

HOPE: Mike, I love you. I do. I love you. You have to love me back because I love you, and I have to say it out loud. I tried waiting and waiting didn't work. I had to say it out loud.

STAN: Michael, go to your room. Look at this mess. All of this. You— (*Pointing at* TESSA) —you are a messy person, and you are infecting my house with your mess. It is time for you to go. And you (*To* HOPE) I don't know who you are—and you (*To* LIZ). This is getting to know each other. You want to get to know each other, Liz? This is what there is to know. And you (*To* MIKE) you are just asking for it. Go to your room.

MIKE: You can't talk to me like that anymore. You can't tell me what to do and when to leave and none of this is my fault, and you can't talk to me like I'm not real. Because I am. I am real.

STAN: Just calm down, Michael. Settle and calm— DOWN.

MIKE: SHUT UP—I'm real. And I know something. Something you can't touch.

STAN: What are you talking about?

MIKE: I'm not telling you.

STAN: Go back to Vassar and learn Italian or whatever the fuck it is I'm paying for. Jesus. You think you can go off to that college and come home and make everyone jump at your command? Well, you can't. I don't care what you know. This is my house. I worked for it. You go work for something. Be a man.

MIKE: Fuck you.

(*Everyone stares at* MIKE. *This is most unexpected.*)

STAN: What did you say to me?

TESSA: I think he said "Fuck you".

candy, candy, candy

HOPE: At the Triple Happiness. A bar in Chinatown. (*Assuming the character of Candy.*) The kind of love between me and Jamie, it's the kind that really messes with you. It is rare. It is the kind of love where you're linked, bonded, you're soulmates, and you just think of the person and then there he is, on the platform of the West 4th Street subway station just because you were thinking of each other. It's the kind of love where you're always inside each other's hearts and minds and cannot stop touching one another's bodies and sleep curled up inside each other like little animals—and I wake up and just watch him breathe, that's enough, and we tickle one another and buy underwear at K-mart and sing made-up songs about kitty-cats, and waste all our time, just waste it, loving each other. Once you've had that, you're sorta ruined for anything else. And I know all about it because I am Candy. Candy like the kind you eat, melts in your mouth but not in your hands. And Jamie, who was my boyfriend, comes back after having been away for a whole year, and he loves me too, just like in all the songs and movies. And this is my story. Even though you think it's something else.

(*Lights up on* JAMIE *at a payphone in the rain.*)

JAMIE: Hey Kid it's me. The guy from the bus. Um.. I hope you're getting this. But, uh, yeah... Hey, Kid from the Bus, you want to come meet me at the Triple Happiness and let me buy you a beer or something? Cause you were kinda right. I could kinda use a friend. Just about now.

HOPE: He calls Candy from a payphone like he used to when he was younger and drunk and calling after a bad fight. They make a date. He's gonna see her. He thinks about it all day, and then he doesn't show,

leaving her waiting at the Triple Happiness. Alone.
And Candy's pissed. She has a right to be, after a
whole year and then getting stood up at the Triple
Happiness. He calls again and tries to explain but
Candy says, "We are all just sitting around waiting for
you to be the person you came here to be. How long
is it gonna take!?" And he goes away and drinks and
sulks and spends all his money, and calls up that kid
he met on the bus because at this point, he needs a
shoulder to cry on, even if he is a guy.

at the triple happiness

(JAMIE *and* MIKE *at the Triple Happiness.* HOPE *follows in
a raincoat. she sits in a corner of the bar with dark glasses
and a wig or a hat. They do not see her, do not notice as
she writes things down in a notebook. She is not quite close
enough to hear everything they say.*)

MIKE: I said "Fuck you" to my dad.

JAMIE: So?

MIKE: So!? So!? So that is a really big deal. And I'm in
love.

JAMIE: Yeah? You're in love?

MIKE: Totally. Dangerously. Wildly. She's 40 and an
alcoholic and she has some weird friendship with my
parents that I totally don't understand. But she loves
me. I know she does. She hasn't said it. But she does.
And we're like soul mates in this very kind of weird,
unsaid, kind of messed up way. And I think about her
all the time and I think about her skin and her laugh.
She smokes cigarettes. I hate cigarettes. I hate alcohol.
I mean, I like bars. But I hate drinking. But I kind of
like this scotch. Maybe if I hang out with her, I'll grow
to like drinking. Scotch and martinis and whatever.
She's...are you ready for this? She's...I can't tell you

who she is. She's kind of...famous. I think that's why she's...you know, about us.

JAMIE: Well, good for you, Kid. That's great. Good for you.

(JAMIE *looks miserable.*)

MIKE: How are you?

JAMIE: Not so good.

MIKE: You don't look so good. I mean, you really don't look good.

JAMIE: I'm fucked. That's how I am. Just fucked. Candy won't see me. I can't see her. I came all this way. I'm staying at the goddamned Y in Brooklyn.

MIKE: You wanna come to my house? We're having a really big holiday thing. I'm sure it would be okay.

do something

LIZ: I want you to leave.

STAN: I thought you wanted me to fight with you.

LIZ: Fighting didn't work. Now I want you to leave.

STAN: I'm not leaving.

LIZ: Fine. I will then.

STAN: Why are you leaving?

LIZ: Somebody has to do something.

STAN: But... It's Christmas.

LIZ: We're Jews, Stanley.

(MIKE *enters with* JAMIE *in tow.*)

MIKE: Everyone, this is Jamie. I met him on the bus. Jamie, this everyone.

(*Everyone looks up and stares. Blackout*)

what do you ache for?

HOPE: What do you mean you never called her? In my story, you call Candy. Twice.

JAMIE: I can't. It won't work. I don't want it.

HOPE: What do you mean you don't want it?

JAMIE: I guess I don't want it bad enough.

HOPE: That's not true.

JAMIE: How do you know what's true?

HOPE: Because I do, that's all. I do because I do. It's a special talent of mine. And what you just said was bullshit. You ache for her. You ache for a real life. You ache for a home.

JAMIE: How do you know what I ache for?

HOPE: I told you. It is my talent.

JAMIE: What do *you* ache for?

HOPE: Oh. I can't tell you that.

JAMIE: Why not?

HOPE: I don't know you very well.

JAMIE: But I know you. Unsent letters to Mike. "Oh, Mike. If we are meant to see each other—"

HOPE: This is none of your business.

JAMIE: Really?

HOPE: Yes, really. It's all going to work out. Me and Mike. You and Candy. Everyone. In the Bad Reality, things and bars and fear mess everything up. But in the Good Reality, nothing can keep true love from realizing itself. Even lovers.

JAMIE: Sometimes it doesn't happen that way.

HOPE: No. You're just scared. Things and bars and fear.

JAMIE: Maybe.

HOPE: But I know.

JAMIE: I see.

HOPE: Do you? Do you see?

JAMIE: Yeah. I think I do.

HOPE: What do you see exactly?

JAMIE: I'm not saying just yet. I see. But I'm not saying.

HOPE: I don't think I like you.

JAMIE: Sure you do. You just don't like that I know things too. You know things. And I know things too. In some ways, you and me are a lot a like.

HOPE: Well, who cares what you know!? And who even invited you here anyway!

JAMIE: You did.

(Beat. HOPE knows JAMIE is right.)

HOPE: Do you think we need a new world?

JAMIE: I do.

HOPE: Are you prepared to give up what you cling to? Are you willing to be truly happy? Even if it's terrifying?

JAMIE: Yes. I am. Are you?

(HOPE, to the audience.)

HOPE: Forge new paths. Make commitments. Be an agent of change. Hold the truth inside yourself. Eat good food. Love the body, the Earth, the people, yourself. Really love yourself. Tell the truth, the whole truth and nothing but the truth so help you God, but only to yourself. If you tell the truth to yourself, you can say whatever you want to other people. It is time. It is time now. Let's go.

let's go

(TESSA *tries sneaking out of the house.*)

MIKE: Where are you going?

TESSA: Back.

MIKE: I'm going with you.

TESSA: No. You're not.

MIKE: Yes! I am! I choose you!

TESSA: Don't you get it, Honey? I'm not one of the choices.

MIKE: *(Not willing to listen)* Let's go back to my room. Right now.

TESSA: No.

MIKE: Please?

TESSA: This isn't a good time. I have a car coming.

MIKE: Come on.

TESSA: Not now. 'Kay?

MIKE: BUT I AM IN LOVE WITH YOU. I AM WILDLY PASSIONATELY IN LOVE WITH EVERY SINGLE THING ABOUT YOU. WHICH WORD DO YOU NOT UNDERSTAND?

TESSA: I'm tired, Honey. Go be in love with Hope.

(MIKE *goes to* HOPE.)

MIKE: No.

HOPE: What do you mean, "No"?

MIKE: Look, I think you're kinda, I mean, I know you have a bad home life and whatever—

HOPE: Leave my home life out of this. I am here for you.

MIKE: You're here for yourself.

HOPE: I have a vision.

MIKE: You have a bad home life.

HOPE: Okay. Let's level. Your family wants you dead. Well not literally dead. But they have no interest in you as a person. They just want to use you to reinforce their own beliefs. They want to suck off your life-force and use it to fuel their system. It is your job to leave. You must leave. Do you see what I am offering you?

MIKE: I think you're weird.

HOPE: That is just not the point! What are you going to choose?

MIKE: Look, I don't know what you're talking about. Ever. I don't ever know what you're talking about. And I think you might need help. I have stuff to do here.

HOPE: Like what? Stuff to do like what?

MIKE: Can you go now? You make me uncomfortable.

HOPE: Stuff to do like love people who can't see you? Stuff to do like watch your parents eat each other up every day and tell you how the world's sorry and unfair but has to be that way just because? Stuff to do like be who everyone else tells you to be without ever once taking in how truly unhappy and hungry you are and that you could, you could, step outside all the rules and be who you are inside? STUFF TO DO LIKE WHAT?

MIKE: I don't know. Maybe all of that.

(*Finally,* HOPE *gets it.*)

HOPE: Oh. Oh, I see.
I do. I see.
And it's Fiction One.
I sit next to you in Fiction One.

the remains

(Daybreak. TESSA *sneaks out of* STAN *and* LIZ's *house.* LIZ *catches her.)*

TESSA: I'm going back.

LIZ: Back where?

TESSA: Back wherever.

LIZ: Can I go with you?

TESSA: With me how?

LIZ: I would like to feed you. Are you hungry? No? Would you put your head in my lap? Oh, no that sounds ridiculous. But…I would like to take care of you. Put you some place warm and make sure that you're fed and good and safe. And I'd like to look at your tattoo some more. And maybe you'd take me to get one of my own. And we could just be together. And, I don't even know, be good. Do you want to be good with me?

TESSA: Say goodbye for me. *(She leaves.)*

the new world

HOPE: Now we can go. And it'll be great. I mean, it'll be real. It'll have problems. But it'll be great.

(A man is with her. We think it's MIKE. *But it turns out to be* JAMIE.)*

JAMIE: I'm ready. Exhausted and ready.

HOPE: Exactly.

(HOPE and JAMIE *face forward.)*

JAMIE: I want this.

HOPE: I know.

JAMIE: You do too.

HOPE: I do.

JAMIE: And we enter together?

HOPE: I think so. Although I'm not too clear on that part. I don't know how much the whole together thing matters.

It occurs to me this isn't about having one another.

JAMIE: So here we go.

HOPE: Yes. Here we go.

(They face out.)

END OF PLAY